Thought of the Day
Thirty-Day Devotional

THOUGHT OF THE DAY THIRTY-DAY DEVOTIONAL

WILLIAM A. CURRY, JR.

CONTENTS

PREFACE

Welcome!

This daily devotional is designed to help anyone who finds themselves hopeless or in need of reassurance that everything will be okay.

We as mankind can find ourselves in hard positions in life. Many times in those positions, we don't know where to turn to or who to turn to. This devotional is a reminder of who God is to us as well as what God will do for us while using us to do it.

This Thirty-Day plus one Devotional is a "hope jump-starter" to get you refocused on the goodness of God as well as assure you that God is with you and working out all things on your behalf. May you find what you need as you read this daily devotional. May you continue to *Trust God*. May God continue to bless you.

OPENING PRAYER

Dear Heavenly Father, I come to You on the behalf of the individual who has chosen to take this thirty-day journey.

Father, I ask that You bless them, give them clarity, and divine guidance into whatever or wherever they need to go.

Lord, I thank You in advance for what You are about to do in their lives.

Father, I thank You for this opportunity to come alongside this reader seeking You, searching for the answers that only You can give.

So again, thank You Heavenly Father.

It is in Jesus' name I pray.

Amen.

DAY 1: FOUR P'S FROM GOD

Thought of the Day

God has placed in you purpose, power, perseverance, and promise. When you trust God, He also gives you the push to obtain and possess your destiny. Trust the push from God. He knows the direction in which you need to go! Trust God.

Daily Scripture

"Have I not commanded you? Be strong and of good courage; do not be afraid, nor be dismayed, for the Lord your God is with you wherever you go." Joshua 1:9

Prayer

Heavenly Father, I come to You asking that You guide me today. That I see in myself what it is You have placed in me. You have given me purpose, power and caused me to persevere. I thank You for Your promises and that You will always be with me. So today, God, please give me clarity to fulfill Your plan for my life.

In Jesus' name, I pray.

Amen.

Your Turn

How does today's thought help your thoughts for today?

DAY 2: MAN'S TRIALS GOD'S TRIUMPH

Thought of the Day

Trusting in God does not mean you won't have trials and tribulations. It does mean as you go through the trials and tribulations God will be with you, and He is the one who gets you through. Remember, Jesus told the disciples, "let us go to the other side." The storm did not stop them. So trust God because this storm won't stop you. Trust God.

Daily Scripture

"These things I have spoken to you, that in Me you may have peace. In the world you will have tribulation; but be of good cheer, I have overcome the world." John 16:33

Prayer

Heavenly Father I come to You, thanking You that You will always be with me. That in these trying times, You walk right alongside me making it possible for me to make it through. I am thankful that I can have peace in these trials and tribulations, because Jesus has overcome the world and these trials and tribulations. Lord, let me not forget that Your hands are upon me and that I will make it through.

In Jesus' name I pray.

Amen.

Your Turn

How does today's thought help your thoughts for today?

DAY 3: DISCERNMENT

Thought of the Day

Ministry is much like life – lonely but fulfilling. We all need help, but not everyone's help is what you need. Ask God who to reach out to, yet it has to be a God thing, not my thing! Trust God! He knows who is needed.

Daily Scripture

"Then Ananias answered, 'Lord, I have heard from many about this man, how much harm he has done to Your saints in Jerusalem. And here he has authority from the chief priests to bind all who call on Your name.' But the Lord said to him, 'Go, for he is a chosen vessel of Mine to bear My name before Gentiles, kings, and the children of Israel.'" Acts 9:13-14

Prayer

Heavenly Father, I come to You seeking Your guidance in who I should be in covenant with. Lord, who I should be in relationships with regarding our lives, ministry, business, and close relationships? Lord, lead me to the right people who encourage me. Lead me to people who help me, lead me to people who stretch me. Lord, I want to be a better person, so place people in my life who let me be the best as I strive to do Your will, Your work, Your way.

In Jesus' name I pray.

Amen.

Your Turn

How does today's thought help your thoughts for today?

DAY 4: BREAKTHROUGH

Thought of the Day

Setbacks are never welcomed yet the breakthrough is always better. Don't let a detour or a delay be a denial because you did not know how to wait. When the Master Chef is in the kitchen of life trust Him; He is the Master of orchestrating blessing! Trust God.

Daily Scripture

"Do not remember the former things, nor consider the things of old. Behold, I will do a new thing, now it shall spring forth; Shall you not know it? I will even make a road in the wilderness and rivers in the desert." Isaiah 43:18-19

Prayer

Heavenly Father, I come to You seeking You in this time of setback that I may not confuse this situation with my final destination in You; that I remember that You are working on my behalf and that I will break through what I am going through; that I don't focus on what has happened but keep my eyes on what You are doing for me; that You are making new ways and paths in which I shall go.

Lord let me forget what is behind me and seek what's in front of me.

In Jesus' name I pray.

Amen.

Your Turn

How does today's thought help your thoughts for today?

DAY 5: LEARN LIFE LESSONS

Thought of the Day

In all things, there is a lesson to be learned. The question is, "Are you looking to learn the lesson the first time?" Habitual offenders don't learn, and the cost continues to rise. Don't be fooled by yourself, you will have yourself looking foolish. Trust God; He knows the path in which you should go. Trust God.

Daily Scripture

"Therefore whoever hears these sayings of Mine, and does them, I will liken him to a wise man who built his house on the rock: and the rain descended, the floods came, and the winds blew and beat on that house; and it did not fall, for it was founded on the rock. But everyone who hears these sayings of Mine, and does not do them, will be like a foolish man who built his house on the sand: and the rain descended, the floods came, and the winds blew and beat on that house; and it fell. And great was its fall." Matthew 7:24-27

Prayer

Heavenly Father, I come to You asking for the wisdom to follow Your Word. Knowing that in all this there is a lesson to be learned. Lord, I ask that I learn the lesson the first time and that we not have to go through this again. Lord, I want to be likened to the wise man and not the foolish one. Lord, lead me in Your ways and speak into my soul. I have given my life to You; I have placed my trust in Your hands. Please let me glean from Your Word and live according to You, garnering the life lessons I am to learn the first time.

In Jesus' name I pray.

Amen.

Your Turn

How does today's thought help your thoughts for today?

DAY 6: YOUR BLESSINGS WILL COME

Thought of the Day

Never be envious or jealous when you see someone being blessed. Celebrate with them. You did not see what they had to endure to receive the blessings they are now getting. Many go to the store to get the olive oil, but many don't see the crushing the olive had to endure for you to get that oil. God is not a respecter of a person; what He does for one He can do for another. Trust God

Daily Scripture

"Nevertheless you have done well that you shared in my distress. Now you Philippians know also that in the beginning of the gospel, when I departed from Macedonia, no church shared with me concerning giving and receiving but you only. For even in Thessalonica you sent aid once and again for my necessities. Not that I seek the gift, but I seek the fruit that abounds to your account. Indeed I have all and abound. I am full, having received from Epaphroditus the things sent from you, a sweet-smelling aroma, an acceptable sacrifice, well pleasing to God. And my God shall supply all your need according to His riches in glory by Christ Jesus." Philippians 4:14-19

Prayer

Heavenly Father, I come to You asking You to calm my emotions as I can, at times, be envious of others or of their season of life. Lord, I do not know most of the time what someone has had to endure to get to where they are in life. I ask You to help me be content with where I am in the process of receiving Your blessings, knowing that You are not partial to anyone and that what You have done for someone else You will do for me. Thank you, God, for being a God who is looking to bless everyone, and that includes me. So again, Lord, please give me peace and the ability to wait for my blessing how you would want me to wait.

In Jesus' name I pray.

Amen.

Your Turn

How does today's thought help your thoughts for today?

DAY 7: YOU HAVE MORE IN YOU

Thought of the Day

One is called to more than what one sees. There will be people who walk out. There will be those who say they are with you but support someone else. Just keep trusting God. He will place you where He predestined you to be. Trust God.

Daily Scripture

"I can do all things through Christ who strengthens me." Philippians 4:13

Prayer

Heavenly Father, I come to You with a spirit of thanks. Thank You for reassuring me that I can do all things through Christ who strengthens me. Thank You for reassuring me that it is not in my strength that I have to this is but in the strength of Jesus Christ that I will accomplish this task at hand. Thank You for reassuring me that you, God, are working things out in my favor–selecting the right people, the right position, the right doors in my path in order that I shall fulfill what my divine destiny is according to Your will. Thank you, Lord, for the many blessings You have in store for me.

In Jesus' name I pray.

Amen.

Your Turn

How does today's thought help your thoughts for today?

DAY 8: TRANSITION

Thought of the Day

Transition is a part of this thing we call life. Don't let hate fuel your transition. You will run out of gas and burn bridges along the way. Seek God in your moves, and you will always make it to your destiny which is your destination. Trust God.

Daily Scripture

"The end of a thing is better than its beginning; The patient in spirit is better than the proud in spirit. Do not hasten in your spirit to be angry, For anger rests in the bosom of fools. Do not say, "Why were the former days better than these?" For you do not inquire wisely concerning this." Ecclesiastes 7:8-10

Prayer

Heavenly Father, I come to You seeking Your help in my transition. As I navigate this transition, I ask for Your peace that surpasses all understanding. I ask that You overshadow me in this time of my life for it is not easy, and I find myself becoming angered easily. I find myself becoming agitated easily. I find myself being hopeless and in need of You. I know I can do this but I can only do this how you want me to by having You lead and guide me through. So Lord, I seek You in this, and I give You all glory of leading me through this transition of my life.

In Jesus' name I pray.

Amen.

Your Turn

How does today's thought help your thoughts for today?

DAY 9: GOD GETS US THROUGH

Thought of the Day

As the days pass by, this old world just isn't the same, yet I trust in the Creator who knows what He is doing. Not that everything will be easy, but God gets me through. So I know He will get you through, too! Trust God.

Daily Scripture

"Jesus answered them, "Do you now believe? Indeed the hour is coming, yes, has now come, that you will be scattered, each to his own, and will leave Me alone. And yet I am not alone, because the Father is with Me. These things I have spoken to you, that in Me you may have peace. In the world you will have tribulation; but be of good cheer, I have overcome the world." John 16:31-33

Prayer

Heavenly Father, I come to You thanking You for the foreknowledge Jesus has given us that He has overcome the world, and the peace that we have is the peace He has given us. Lord, I ask that when I start getting worn down with what is going on in this world, You will let me remember what Your Word said, that we will have trials and tribulation, but they are overcome by You. Please let me be steadfast in the promise You have given me.

In Jesus' name I pray.

Amen.

Your Turn

How does today's thought help your thoughts for today?

DAY 10: HELPING HAND

Thought of the Day

Everyone, including Pastors, Supporters, Motivators, and Pushers, is going through something, while still being the Pastors, Supporters, Motivators, and Pushers. Yet God is still in control. Check on them because they need help as well.

Daily Scripture

"Let love be without hypocrisy. Abhor what is evil. Cling to what is good. Be kindly affectionate to one another with brotherly love, in honor giving preference to one another; not lagging in diligence, fervent in spirit, serving the Lord; rejoicing in hope, patient in tribulation, continuing steadfastly in prayer; distributing to the needs of the saints, given to hospitality." Romans 12: 9-13

Prayer

Heavenly Father, I come to You asking that You keep me mindful that others who support me may need my support in my prayers, and at times for me to push and encourage them. God, I ask that when I am praying, I remember to include them in my prayers. I ask that I am not self-centered but that I pray and attend to my helpers as well. God, you have placed these people in my life, and I must keep them covered in prayer as well. God, I know that you can lift them and keep them.

God, I thank you for all that You do.

In Jesus' name I pray.

Amen.

Your Turn

How does today's thought help your thoughts for today?

DAY 11: PRAYER HELPS

Thought of the Day

We all need prayer. It's the prayer that changes things. Your relationship with the Master is key to how your life and future will go. Trust God. He knows what He is doing!

Daily Scripture

"I sought the Lord, and He heard me, And delivered me from all my fears. They looked to Him and were radiant, And their faces were not ashamed. This poor man cried out, and the Lord heard him, And saved him out of all his troubles. The angel of the Lord encamps all around those who fear Him, And delivers them." Psalm 34:4-7

Prayer

Heavenly Father, I seek You now, praying to know that prayer changes things. Lord, give me the wisdom to seek You in all I do, praying to You for what it is You would have me to do. I know that if I do it in my will, it will be messed up; but if I seek Your will, then it will work for my good. I thank You, Lord, that I can come to You in prayer and that in prayer You hear me and the answers which I seek I find because You, O Lord, heard my cries. Lord let me never forget to pray or how to pray because prayer is the difference in the outcome of my life.

In Jesus name I pray.

Amen.

Your Turn

How does today's thought help your thoughts for today?

DAY 12: GOD IS FAITHFUL

Thought of the Day

In this thing called life, God has kept me. He has shown Himself faithful. He has placed faithful people in my life who celebrate me and support me, not just in words, but in actions. So make sure you celebrate those who celebrate you! Be blessed.

Daily Scripture

"But the Lord is faithful, who will establish you and guard you from the evil one. And we have confidence in the Lord concerning you, both that you do and will do the things we command you. Now may the Lord direct your hearts into the love of God and into the patience of Christ." 2 Thessalonians 3:3-5

Prayer

Heavenly Father, I come to You thanking You for always being on my side. Thank You for always helping me, even in times I should not have been helped. I am thankful that You see the best in me, not as man sees me but as You, God, see me. I thank You that You handcrafted me to be this marvelous creation and that You continue to make me better as time goes on. God, I seek You in all aspects of my life, that it will continuously get better because You make it better. Thank You, Lord, for the helpful people You place in my life who represent You. Thank you, Lord for the love they give me to be better. Lord, thank You.

In Jesus' name I pray.

Amen.

Your Turn

How does today's thought help your thoughts for today?

DAY 13: ASSIGNED PUSHER

Thought of the Day

Some are assigned to you yet don't like the assignment, so they make your mission harder. That's their assignment, to make it hard on you and to push you to grow. So thank God for them and love them from afar. After all, Judas ate the last supper and still betrayed Jesus. Trust God.

Daily Scripture

"Repay no one evil for evil. Have regard for good things in the sight of all men. If it is possible, as much as depends on you, live peaceably with all men. Beloved, do not avenge yourselves, but rather give place to wrath; for it is written, 'Vengeance is Mine, I will repay,' says the Lord." Romans 12:17-19

Prayer

Heavenly Father, I come to You seeking your strength in remaining peaceful and in Your spirit. There are people, all the time, who try to pull me into situations that would cause me to not be like You or to operate in a spirit that is not pleasing to You, Lord. I ask, God, that You keep Your arms around me and that You give me the strength to press forward. Lord, give me the wisdom to know how to respond to negative people and situations. As Your Word says, as peacefully as possible let me do exactly that. God, I know there will be some negative people I must deal with. Lord, anoint me with the grace to do so knowing that You, Lord, will take care of them and every situation I may be in.

In Jesus' name I pray.

Amen.

Your Turn

How does today's thought help your thoughts for today?

DAY 14: OBEDIENCE

Thought of the Day

When you do what God gives you to do, you get what God has for you. It may not be in your time, yet His time is always on time. I trust Him because He has never failed me. Trust God; He's got you! Trust God!

Daily Scripture

"If you are willing and obedient, You shall eat the good of the land." Isaiah 1:19

Prayer

Heavenly Father, I come to You through the precious name of Jesus, asking for Your divine presence, so that with Your power I can fulfill the task You have placed before me. I'm asking for Your divine presence so that I can obey all of Your requirements to accomplish what You have set out for me to do. Father, I know in my obedience to You I shall receive what You have for me!

In Jesus' name I pray.

Amen.

Your Turn

How does today's thought help your thoughts for today?

DAY 15: USED BY GOD

Thought of the Day

There are divine moments God places you in, not for *you* but for someone else who is in need. You are the representative of God for that moment. Thank God for choosing you and thank God for filling you with what that individual needed at that time. It's a God thing! Trust God.

Daily Scripture

"Now Hannah spoke in her heart; only her lips moved, but her voice was not heard. Therefore Eli thought she was drunk. So Eli said to her, 'How long will you be drunk? Put your wine away from you!' But Hannah answered and said, 'No, my lord, I am a woman of sorrowful spirit. I have drunk neither wine nor intoxicating drink, but have poured out my soul before the Lord. Do not consider your maidservant a wicked woman, for out of the abundance of my complaint and grief I have spoken until now.' Then Eli answered and said, 'Go in peace, and the God of Israel grant your petition which you have asked of Him.'" 1 Samuel 1:13-17

Prayer

Heavenly Father, I come thanking You for placing me in the right places to be Your ambassador. I thank You as well for placing others in my path to be Your ambassador. God, I ask that You always fill me up with what to say and do, as I know You give to those whom You send to me, equipped with what it is I need. Lord, please always grant me a hearing ear so I can truly be a help in all matters which are before me. Lord, grant me the words to say when You send someone to help me, God, I ask that You always will be in the midst of whatever position I am in. Whether it is receiving or giving, I must be guided by You.

It's in Jesus' name I pray.

Amen.

Your Turn

How does today's thought help your thoughts for today?

DAY 16: WORSHIP OVER WORRY

Thought of the Day

When you worry, you cause emotional stress on your physical being. Yet, when you worship, you call God to free you from your worry. It's better to worship than to worry! God is freeing you, the enemy is trying to cage you. Be free! Trust God.

Daily Scripture

"Look at the birds of the air, for they neither sow nor reap nor gather into barns; yet your heavenly Father feeds them. Are you not of more value than they? Which of you by worrying can add one cubit to his stature? So why do you worry about clothing? Consider the lilies of the field, how they grow: they neither toil nor spin; and yet I say to you that even Solomon in all his glory was not arrayed like one of these." Matthew 6:26-29

Prayer

Heavenly Father, I seek You asking that You calm my storms. That whatever I am worried about, You take that worry from me. God, You show me how to make it through this storm. Lord, that reminds me that what is a surprise to me is no shock to You. Lord, please let me worship and not worry. Let me be reminded that You care for the birds of the air and flowers in the fields so I should know that You will take care of me. God, thank You for taking time to make me special and since I am specially made, You will provide for me.

In Jesus' name I pray.

Amen.

Your Turn

How does today's thought help your thoughts for today?

DAY 17: THE SOURCE

Thought of the Day

God is never the resource but is always the Source. A resource will run out, but the Source never runs out. The Source creates a new resource when one resource runs dry. God is the source of all resources who, if you ask Him, will provide you with a new resource when one is no longer an option. Trust God.

Daily Scripture

"Indeed I have all and abound. I am full, having received from Epaphroditus the things sent from you, a sweet-smelling aroma, an acceptable sacrifice, well pleasing to God. And my God shall supply all your need according to His riches in glory by Christ Jesus. Now to our God and Father be glory forever and ever. Amen." Philippians 4:18-20

Prayer

Heavenly Father, I thank You for always being my source, no matter what happens or what runs out. God, I know You never run out of anything. God, I ask that You lead me to new streams and resources before resources become scarce. I know, Lord, that I am blessed, and because I am blessed I am supposed to be a blessing. I know all things I shall receive may not be material, some may be spiritual. So again, Lord, thank

You for Your guiding hand and always being my source.

In Jesus' name I pray.

Amen.

Your Turn

How does today's thought help your thoughts for today?

DAY 18: LOW PLACES

Thought of the Day

God is amazing at giving His strength to those who are in a lowly place or space. He holds us while we are in those lowly places and spaces, letting the rebuilding process happen. God is able and willing. Trust God.

Daily Scripture

"Oh, give thanks to the Lord, for He is good! For His mercy endures forever. Let the redeemed of the Lord say so, whom He has redeemed from the hand of the enemy." Psalm 107:1-2

Prayer

Heavenly Father, I come to You saying "thank you" for always holding me, especially when I find myself in low spaces and places of life. God, I thank You that in my times of need You are always there for me, never judging me but holding me. God, You have given me peace in storms and joy in sadness. I thank You, God, for Your never-ending love and hope in me. God, let me always remember that You are on my side and are for me. God, constantly remind me that I am yours, and I can make it through because You are with me.

In Jesus' name I pray.

Amen.

Your Turn

How does today's thought help your thoughts for today?

DAY 19: A WAY OUT

Thought of the Day

The worst place to be locked up in is in one's own mind. See, the only person who can let you free is you. There is no one to let you out: no jailer, no guard, no corrections officer. Only we have the keys to the cell in which we have locked ourselves up. So, when you have a relationship with God, in the times you are starting to go to that self-made cell in your mind, seek God and He will free you. God will keep your doors open and show you the way out. Trust God.

Daily Scripture

"You will keep him in perfect peace whose mind is stayed on You because he trusts in You." Isaiah 26:3

Prayer

Heavenly Father, I come to You, thankful for Your reminder that I can be in perfect peace. I just have to remain focused on You. God, let me be focused on You and the tasks You have given me. God, I know that I can get distracted. I know I can get discouraged when I am not focused on You. I know that things in this world will have me not following You. So I ask, God, that You keep me focused and nudge me when I am starting to drift away from Your lead. Lord, my peace is in You and God, I need my peace. So thank You, God, for holding my peace.

In Jesus' name I pray.

Amen.

Your Turn

How does today's thought help your thoughts for today?

DAY 20: GOD WILL CARRY IT

Thought of the Day

We tend to carry things we are not meant to carry. We carry the baggage of others, we carry past hurts, we carry past failures as if they just happened. It is hard to let go of things, and many times those things won't let go of you. It is okay to empty the baggage, as God will carry you and He frees you from the baggage. Trust God. And as you continue to move forward, give the baggage to Him and pick up His yoke for it is lighter than the baggage. Trust God.

Daily Scripture

"Come to Me, all you who labor and are heavy laden, and I will give you rest. Take My yoke upon you and learn from Me, for I am gentle and lowly in heart, and you will find rest for your souls. For My yoke is easy and My burden is light." Matthew 11:28-30

Prayer

Heavenly Father, I come to You seeking Your help with the load I am carrying. God, I know that if I seek You, You are more than willing to help me carry these heavy-laden burdens. Lord, I can't carry this by myself. In fact, I can't carry it at all. It's too heavy for me to carry at all. God, I know that You are a way-maker and a present help in the time of trouble, so God, please help me bear this burden and give me the strength to make it through. Your Word says that I am more than a conqueror, and I know it is because of You. So thank You, God, for carrying me as You carry this burden I am going through.

In Jesus' name I pray.

Amen.

Your Turn

How does today's thought help your thoughts for today?

DAY 21: REUNION

Thought of the Day

There are times in our lives when people transition from earth to Heaven. When those whom we love transition — be it a mother, father, son, daughter, aunt, uncle, niece, nephew, grandmother, grandfather, or a close or dear friend — we miss them dearly and want them to be back with us here on earth. It is a tough thing to have a loved one pass away. As one who believes in Christ, we know that it is not a goodbye but a "see you later." We know that the loved one is in no more pain or sorrow, yet is in a place that we long to be, too. Knowing God holds our loved ones while they await our arrival brings God's peace to us on earth. Trust God

Daily Scripture

"But I do not want you to be ignorant, brethren, concerning those who have fallen asleep, lest you sorrow as others who have no hope. For if we believe that Jesus died and rose again, even so God will bring with Him those who sleep in Jesus. For this we say to you by the word of the Lord, that we who are alive and remain until the coming of the Lord will by no means precede those who are asleep. For the Lord Himself will descend from heaven with a shout, with the voice of an archangel, and with the trumpet of God. And the dead in Christ will rise first. Then we who are alive and remain shall be caught up together with them in the clouds to meet the Lord in the air. And thus we shall always be with the Lord." 1 Thessalonians 4:13-17

Prayer

Heavenly Father, I come to You with a heavy heart, yet with a heart of hope because Your Word confirms that there will be a reunion with my loved ones who have passed. It is a hard thing to try and understand, yet Lord, I trust You and what You have in store for my love and me. Thank you that one day we shall be reunited, that we shall have a joyous time once again. I am thankful, Lord, that You allow the memories of my loved ones to remain in my mind, which allows them to live on through me. God, thank you for Your love and kindness toward me. Thank you, God, for always being here for me. As much as I am saddened and yet happy because my loved one is with You, I know that my loved one is in the best place anyone could be and that is with You, in Your loving and caring hands. In Jesus' name I pray.
Amen.

Your Turn

How does today's thought help your thoughts for today?

DAY 22: STILL THANKFUL

Thought of the Day

To be thankful does not mean you have not suffered some losses or experienced some hurt. It doesn't mean that life has been easy. It means that even in the losses, hurts, and hard times, God was still blessing you, holding you, caring for you, and at times carrying you. So I am thankful that God never stops being in my corner. Trust God

Daily Scripture

"Rejoice always, pray without ceasing, in everything give thanks; for this is the will of God in Christ Jesus for you." 1 Thessalonians 5:16-18

Prayer

Heavenly Father, I come to You rejoicing and to simply say "thank you." I know it is You who has kept me, and it is You who continues to bless me. So God, thank You for always being with and for me. Thank You for always providing for me. Thank You for always protecting me and most of all thank You for always loving me.

In Jesus' name I pray.

Amen.

Your Turn

How does today's thought help your thoughts for today?

DAY 23: PRAY

Thought of the Day

The days it's hard to pray are the days you should pray the hardest. Just a little talk with Jesus will get you through. Trust God.

Daily Scripture

"Rejoice always, pray without ceasing, in everything give thanks; for this is the will of God in Christ Jesus for you." 1 Thessalonians 5:16-18

Prayer

Heavenly Father, I kneel before You to pray. I know that prayer is my way of communicating with You, Heavenly Father. I know that You want us to continuously pray unto You. As a mother and father want to hear from their children, so do You, God. It is the perpetual conversations which You, God, love to have with Your children. In these conversations we can elicit Your help and You can hear our hearts. That is our communication. All things good or bad, happy or sad, all can be talked about with You. No matter what, God, you won't judge me or put me down or cast me away. God, you will help me and hug me and love me. So God, I thank You for giving us the ability to communicate with You through prayer.

In Jesus' name I pray.

Amen.

Your Turn

How does today's thought help your thoughts for today?

DAY 24: SOURCE

Thought of the Day

God should never be a last resort. God should never be the last to hear about what is going on. God is always the first to know for He is the answer to all things. Don't delay your blessings, breakthrough, healing, or deliverance by keeping God out of the picture! God can do it for you! Trust God.

Daily Scripture

"Ask, and it will be given to you; seek, and you will find; knock, and it will be opened to you. For everyone who asks receives, and he who seeks finds, and to him who knocks it will be opened." Matthew 7:7-8

Prayer

Heavenly Father, I come to You with a thankful heart that You have always been my source and never just a resource. God, no matter what or how long anything took, You never ran out of what it was I needed at that time. God, I am thankful that Your source never runs dry and that when I have a need You have an answer. When I am low You are always able and willing to fill me up. I am thankful to God that before I even know I have a need You already know and are pooling all the resources I need because You are the source for all resources. So again, thank you God, for being my source.

In Jesus' name I pray.

Amen.

Your Turn

How does today's thought help your thoughts for today?

DAY 25: GOD'S STANDARD

Thought of the Day

It's not man's standard to which one should strive to live up to but God's standards. God's standards are possible to obtain. One has to have a relationship with God, and while in the relationship, one finds out what God is wanting for your life. Trust God.

Daily Scripture

"I beseech you therefore, brethren, by the mercies of God, that you present your bodies a living sacrifice, holy, acceptable to God, which is your reasonable service. And do not be conformed to this world, but be transformed by the renewing of your mind, that you may prove what is that good and acceptable and perfect will of God." Romans 12:1-2

Prayer

Heavenly Father, I come to You seeking to do it Your way, not my way. God, I know Your ways are higher than my ways and Your thoughts are higher than my thoughts. God, I seek to get it right, whatever it is You have me for me to do. God, I have tried my way and others' ways, and I have failed in those attempts. But I know that if I do it how You want me to do it, I will not fail because I know, God, that You could never fail.

So doing it Your way is a guaranteed success. Thank You, God, for being willing to help me and guide me in the ways of You and Your standards.

In Jesus' name I pray.

Amen.

Your Turn

How does today's thought help your thoughts for today?

DAY 26: GOD HAS A PLAN

Thought of the Day

Have a plan, work your plan. We set out on different journeys and get lost on the way because we did not have a plan or seek the one who holds our plans of life. One walks aimlessly, wondering "why am I lost?" When we seek Him who knows the plans He has for us, we find what we are supposed to do and be. Trust God.

Daily Scripture

"For I know the thoughts that I think toward you, says the Lord, thoughts of peace and not of evil, to give you a future and a hope. Then you will call upon Me and go and pray to Me, and I will listen to you. And you will seek Me and find *Me*, when you search for Me with all your heart. I will be found by you, says the Lord, and I will bring you back from your captivity; I will gather you from all the nations and from all the places where I have driven you, says the Lord, and I will bring you to the place from which I cause you to be carried away captive." Jeremiah 29:11-14

Prayer

Heavenly Father, I come to You wanting to know what it is You have planned for me in my life. I want to know that God,

I walk in the path in which You have for me to walk. God, I know You have a plan for me. I just don't know it myself, so I seek You. I seek Your guidance for my life. I have tried to make my plans and have failed in carrying them through. I know if I seek You and You give me the plan You have for me, I cannot fail. I will succeed. So God, I am seeking You with my heart and my soul so that You let me know what it is I am designed and called to do and that I bring honor and glory unto You.

In Jesus' name I pray.

Amen.

Your Turn

How does today's thought help your thoughts for today?

DAY 27: FORGIVENESS

Thought of the Day

Forgiveness is a process that one goes through, a process that takes time to go through. So afford yourself the time. Remember as you forgive to also allow yourself to be healed, by seeking God as you forgive. It's His power that will allow you to forgive and heal. Trust God.

Daily Scripture

"Let all bitterness, wrath, anger, clamor, and evil speaking be put away from you, with all malice. And be kind to one another, tenderhearted, forgiving one another, even as God in Christ forgave you." Romans 4:31-32

Prayer

Heavenly Father, I come to You asking You to help me with my forgiveness. And as I forgive the trespasses, I also allow myself to forgive me. I know that it is hard to forgive oneself but God, I know You can guide me through this situation I am in. God, You are the great healer and I know You can heal this pain and allow me to forgive even though it is hard right now for me to forgive. Lord, I don't want to hold or harbor malice or ill feelings toward anyone, for we all are Your creation. God, let me love people as You do, and in doing so I will be able to forgive.

In Jesus' name, I pray.

Amen.

Your Turn

How does today's thought help your thoughts for today?

DAY 28: GRACE

Thought of the Day

We all need grace because we don't know what someone else may be going through. God gives us grace daily, because He knows we need it. So we need to afford others the grace God gives, and we need to afford us the grace we need. Seek God's grace, for His grace never runs out. Trust God.

Daily Scripture

"But He gives more grace. Therefore He says: 'God resists the proud, but gives grace to the humble.'" James 4:6

Prayer

Heavenly Father, please let me remember that You give me grace daily even when I don't deserve it. God, You are always good to me and afford me the space of grace in my daily life as I make mistakes often and many times without knowing that I have made a mistake. God, I ask that You give me the strength and wherewithal to extend that same grace to those who may be having a bad day or to those who may see things differently than I. I know God many times I don't see things as You do and yet, You extend grace to me. So I ask God that You guide me to be more graceful.

In Jesus' name, I pray.

Amen.

Your Turn

How does today's thought help your thoughts for today?

DAY 29: TEARS

Thought of the Day

As one goes through life there will be some tears that flow. There are tears of sadness and of joy. Yet in all of the tears, God is with you. God sees the tears that flow and wants to comfort you through them. God wants to celebrate the good tears and heal the sorrowful ones. God's desire and will is to be with you in both times. For God to be in both seasons of tears one has to let God in. When one lets God in, He can comfort, collect, and release the pain and joys in one's tears. Trust God.

Daily Scripture

"Sing praise to the Lord, you saints of His, And give thanks at the remembrance of His holy name. For His anger is but for a moment, His favor is for life; Weeping may endure for a night, But joy comes in the morning." Psalm 30:4-5

Prayer

Heavenly Father, I come to You asking You to help me through the rainy season in my life. As the tears start to stream down my face, Lord, let me know that You are there with me catching every one as it rolls down. God, I know the tears are not in vain and that every one of them has a purpose behind them. God, please give me the strength to get up and move forward even with the tears flowing. Deposit in my spirit the assurance that the tears will stop and victory is right ahead of me.

In Jesus' name I pray.

Amen.

Your Turn

How does today's thought help your thoughts for today?

DAY 30: GOOD AND BAD DAYS

Thought of the Day

While there are good days and bad days, know that God is in both types of days. That God gives us strength in both days. That God can be found on both days. It's just that on the bad days you have to trust a little harder. Please know when you can't see Him, He is there. When you can't trace Him, He is there. Trust God.

Daily Scripture

"Where can I go from Your Spirit? Or where can I flee from Your presence? If I ascend into heaven, You are there; If I make my bed in hell, behold, You are there. If I take the wings of the morning, And dwell in the uttermost parts of the sea, Even there Your hand shall lead me, And Your right hand shall hold me. If I say, "Surely the darkness shall fall on me," Even the night shall be light about me; Indeed, the darkness shall not hide from You, But the night shines as the day; The darkness and the light are both alike to You." Psalm 139:7-12

Prayer

Heavenly Father, as life goes on, I know that there will be good days and bad days. God, I pray You to guide me through them both. I need You on my good days and even more on the bad days. I know in the bad days, they won't be so bad or unbearable because You will be on my side, guiding me through. I thank you, God, that Your Word says "You will never leave me nor forsake me" meaning that You will always be with me. God, I'm sure that my bad days won't last forever and neither will my good days. Yet am hopeful because in them both You are with me and You will last forever.

In Jesus' name I pray.

Amen.

Your Turn

How does today's thought help your thoughts for today?

DAY 31: HOPE

Thought of the Day

Sometimes we will feel as there is no hope and the future looks bleak, no way out. That it is time to throw in the towel and give up. That I am finished, and the only thing left to do is give up, give in, give out, and end it all. God says when your strength is no more, when you have no more fight in you, when you throw in the towel, God will throw it back to you and say "wipe off the sweat; we have just begun." That your might is not greater than My might, that your power is no match to My Power, and that in any situation you may be in, know that I am God and I am the God of all situations who can get you through. That I am the fighter who you need to fight for you. So hold on and Trust me for I will finish this and it shall work out in your favor. Don't lose hope. Trust God!

Daily Scripture

"And Moses said to the people, "Do not be afraid. Stand still, and see the salvation of the Lord, which He will accomplish for you today. For the Egyptians whom you see today, you shall see again no more forever. The Lord will fight for you, and you shall hold your peace." Exodus 14:13-14

Prayer

Heavenly Father, I come to You seeking help and hope, for

I am at the end of my rope and don't know how am going to make it through this. God, I know You are able and willing to help me, and I am asking right now that You do so. I know I cannot do it by my power. God, You are all-powerful, and there is nothing You cannot do. I place this situation in Your hands, and I bow to asking that You, God, let hope rise in me. Let hope spring forth as a rushing river springs forth. Lord, You are my hope; and with You, I know victory is mine and I shall make it through. Please God, let me remember that all I need to do is trust You, and You will get me through.

In Jesus' name I pray.

Amen.

Your Turn

How does today's thought help your thoughts for today?

DEDICATION - HELEN CURRY

Helen Jewel (Ford) Curry was the wife of William A. Curry, Sr, and mother to eight children, including me.

My mother was a homemaker for most of her life. She would care for our home so well; it was a gift that God anointed her with. She would care for her family seamlessly while dealing with her issues. Dealing with nine different attitudes sometimes daily; you know, a husband and eight children can be a handful.

What I noticed about my mother was that while going through her daily tasks, she would pray. Sometimes the prayer would be one-word prayers like "Lord" or sometimes more elaborate prayers. Yet in all times and trials, she was a prayer warrior.

As she has transitioned from her work here on to glory with our Heavenly Father, it was impressed on me to write this thirty-day devotional to remind us all, that in all we go through, no matter what, with prayer we can make it through as we seek and trust God.

MEET WILL

Pastor William A. Curry, Jr. is the Senior Pastor of New Beginnings Church, Fort Wayne, Indiana.

He was born in Detroit Michigan on June 4, 1979, to William and Helen Curry. Dr. Curry comes from a large family, having seven siblings. He graduated from East Detroit High school in 1998. In August of 1998, Dr. Curry enlisted in the United States Marine Corps. While in the service, Dr. Curry served in many different capacities, from being a Truck Driver, Recruiter, Instructor, Operations Chief, Logistics Chief, to ending his career as Motor Transportation

Operations Chief. His work spanned more than 17 years of service. During his service, Dr. Curry traveled to 24 different countries and 42 of the 50 states in the United States.

Dr. Curry was always, from childhood, curious about God and His Church. Dr. Curry was 13 years of age when he started actively seeking God. Dr. Curry started going to Bible Studies with a neighbor who was a Jehovah's Witness, seeking to find out more about who God was. Eventually, Dr. Curry's home church growing up was Israel Missionary Baptist Church in Detroit, Michigan, where the Pastor was the late Rev Samuel S. Jenkins, whose predecessor is Dr. Edward McCree. Dr. Curry searched different denominations in his search which always led him back to Jesus Christ.

Dr. Curry and his family joined The Sanctuary of Jacksonville (SOJ) in December, 2010. While attending, Dr. Curry became active in the Church by joining the Usher team. While Dr. Curry was serving on the Usher team, he was selected to become an Armorbearer which was a group of men in the church to selected to attend to the Pastor. While serving as an Armorbearer, Dr. Curry began his education in Biblical studies, attending North Carolina College of Theology. He received his Associate's Degree in 2013 in Biblical Studies. After he deployed to Afghanistan, Dr. Curry continued his studies at North Carolina College of Theology, receiving his Bachelor Degree in Biblical Studies in 2014.

While in Afghanistan, Dr. Curry accepted the calling on his life on January 13, 2014. Dr. Curry "believes God had to get him by himself so He could talk to him". Dr. Curry was a leader in the Church in Afghanistan, again filling the role as head Armorbearer to Dr. Jeffery Davidson from January to May of 2014. After returning home, Dr. Curry was ordained June 17, 2014, by Dr. Jonathan L. Cook, Senior Pastor of The Sanctuary of Jacksonville, who is also Dr. Curry's Spiritual father.

Dr. Curry became the Head Armorbearer at the Sanctuary of Jacksonville and Overseer of all Men's Ministries, Ushers, Watchmen, and Parking Lot ministries until he retired from the Marine Corps in October, 2014. Dr. Curry asked the Lord where He wanted him, and God led him to Fort Wayne, Indiana where Dr. Curry started Fort Wayne Community Church on January 7, 2015. Dr. Curry continued his education and received his Master's in Theology in 2016 and his Doctorate in Theology in 2017, both from North Carolina College of Theology. Dr. Curry reached out to the Senior Pastor of New Beginnings Church, and the two churches merged. Dr. Curry transitioned from working at Noble County Probation as their substance abuse and cognitive behavior instructor in 2018 and became one of the many chaplains at Parkview Regional Medical Center.

Dr. Curry is married to Caletta L. Curry and they have six children: Elisha, Ja Shawn, Addonus, Andrea, Jocelyn, and Xeriah.

ACKNOWLEDGEMENTS

I want to thank God for giving me hope in the storm of life I was in. In that time, He gave me the ability to capture my thoughts and prayers and be able to put them first on Facebook and then on paper.

Thank you to my wife, Caletta, who encouraged me to write and supports me in all my endeavors.

My friend and encourager, Patrick Reicke, who proofread and encouraged me as I wrote this book.

A huge thank you to Dr. Jon Swanson and Hope Swanson Smith for editing and helping me make this book possible. Without them I would have been lost.

All of you made this book possible. So again, thank you.

Will